The Whale

for Diane and Michael

This book has been reviewed
for accuracy by

Carroll R. Norden, Ph.D.
Professor of Zoology
University of Wisconsin—Milwaukee

Copyright © 1991 Steck-Vaughn Company

Copyright © 1979, Raintree Publishers Limited Partnership

Library of Congress Number: 79-13379

    11 12 13 14 W   99 98 97 96 95

Library of Congress Cataloging in Publication Data

Hogan, Paula Z
  The whale.

  Cover title: The life cycle of the whale.
  SUMMARY: Describes in simple terms the life cycle of the whale.
  1. Whales—Juvenile literature. [1. Whales]
I. Halt, Karen. II. Title. III. Title: The life cycle of the whale.
QL737.C4H63 599'.51 79-13379
ISBN 0-8172-1500-X hardcover library binding
ISBN 0-8114-8180-8 softcover binding

The
WHALE

By Paula Z. Hogan
Illustrations by Karen Halt

RSVP

RAINTREE
STECK-VAUGHN
P U B L I S H E R S
The Steck-Vaughn Company

Austin, Texas

The Whale

Humpback whales live in the sea but are not fish. They breathe air and stay warm in the coldest weather.

Blubber is a thick layer of fat. It keeps the whales warm. When they have no food, whales can live off their blubber.

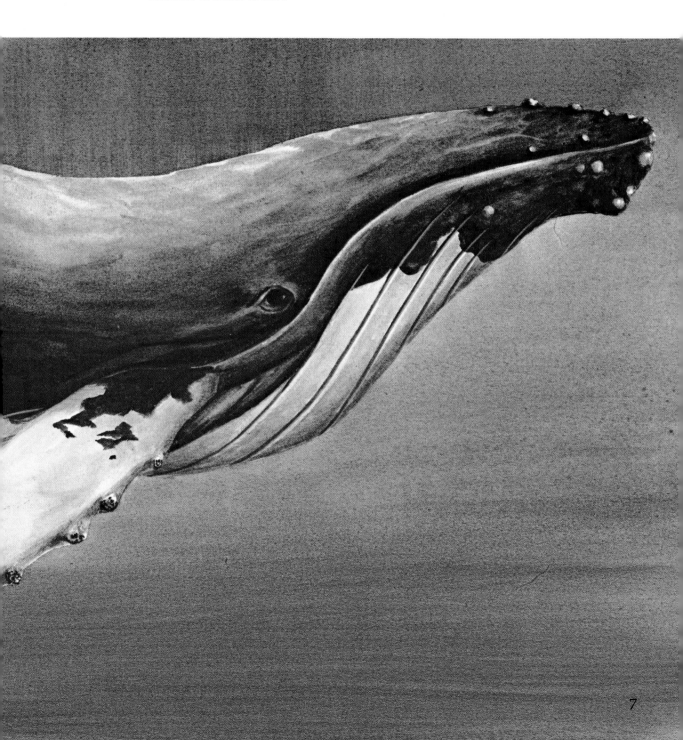

Most great whales don't need teeth. They eat very small animals called krill.

Krill live in icy water near the North and South Poles. Whales feed all summer long. Their mouths can hold a ton of krill!

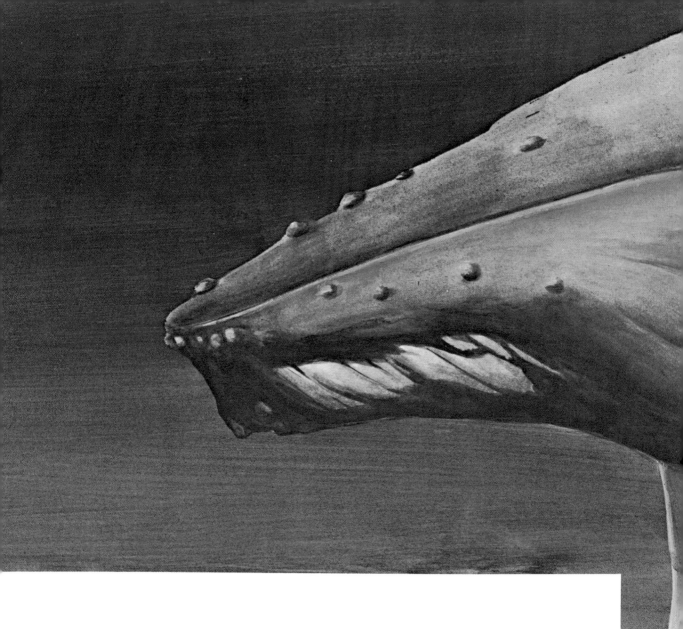

Whales can't see or smell very
well. How do they find food?

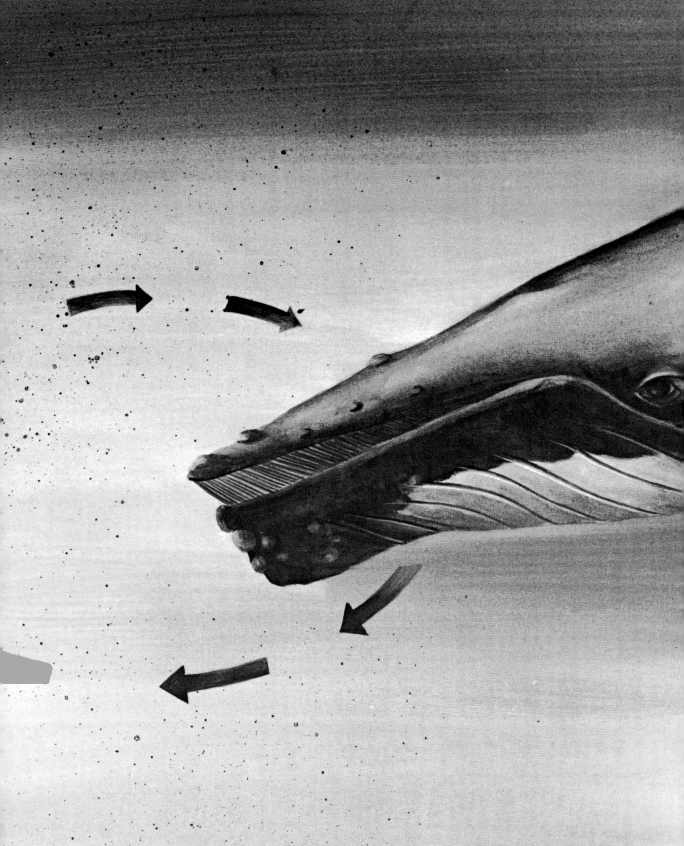

Whales make a clicking sound,
then listen for the echo. The echo
tells them where to find krill.

Side fins work to steer, dive, and stop. The tail fins push the whale along. Whales like to jump out of the water and fall back with a splash.

Whales can stay underwater a long time. Then they stay above water for a few minutes before diving down again.

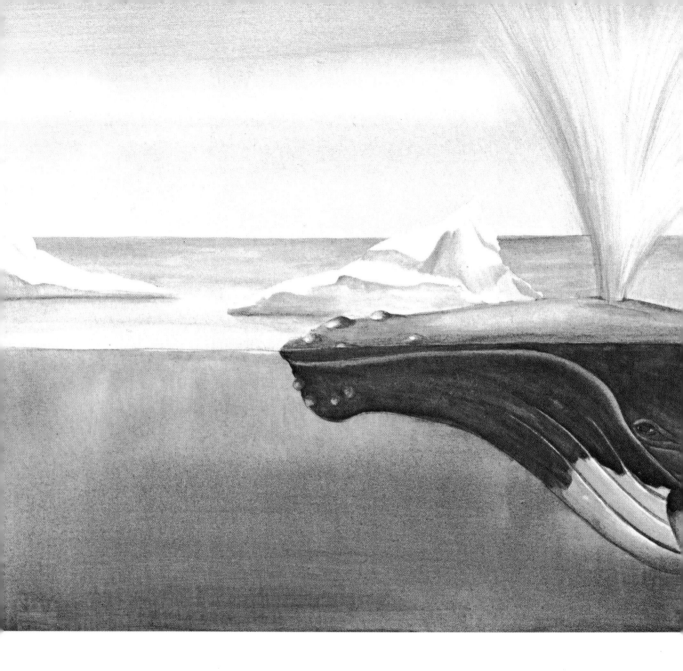

They breathe through a hole on the top of their heads. When they blow out, a small cloud forms.

In winter whales swim to warmer waters. They go together in large herds. Year after year each herd comes back to the same place.

Baby whales are born in early winter. Like many land animals, mother whales give milk to their babies.

By summer the babies have
grown a layer of blubber. Then the
herd heads for colder water to
eat krill.

Every year there are fewer
whales. Many are hunted for their
blubber and meat. Soon there may
be no whales at all.

narwhal

dolphin

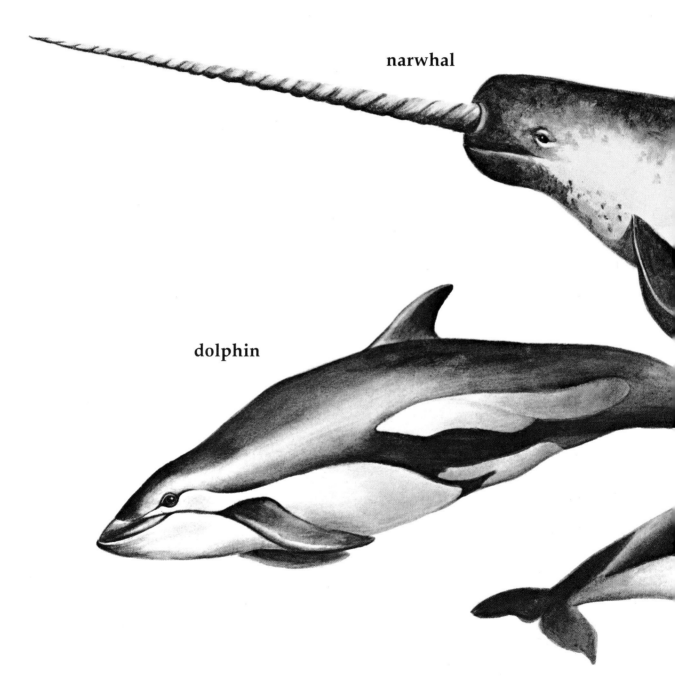

Other animals live in the sea, breathe air, and give milk to their babies. Some are dolphins, porpoises, and narwhals. None of these grow bigger than whales. Whales are the biggest animals of all.

porpoise

GLOSSARY

These words are explained the way they are used in this book. Words of more than one syllable are in parentheses. The heavy type shows which syllable is stressed.

blubber (**blub**·ber) — layer of fat under the skin of a whale

dolphin (**dol**·phin) — a small whale with a long beak

echo (**ech**·o) — the repeating of a sound

fin — part of a whale's body that sticks out and moves

great whales — the largest kinds of whales

herd — a group of whales

humpback (**hump**·back) — a kind of great whale that has long side fins

krill — small shrimplike animals that whales eat

layer (**lay**·er) — an outer covering

porpoise (**por**·poise) — a small whale with a short beak

narwhal (**nar**·whal) — a small whale with a long tusk

ton — weighs two thousand pounds